About This Book

Title: *Journey Through the City*

Step: 5

Word Count: 224

Skills in Focus: Long vowel e spelled y and ey

Tricky Words: neighborhoods, outside, yard, animals, people, center, gather, between

Ideas for Using This Book

Before Reading:

- **Comprehension:** Look at the title and cover image together. Walk through the pictures in the book with readers and have them make predictions about what they might learn while reading. Help them make connections by asking what they already know about cities.
- **Accuracy:** Practice saying the tricky words listed on page 1.
- **Phonics:** Tell readers they will read words with long vowel sounds. Explain that *y* and *ey* make the long vowel sound /e/. Have students look at the title of this book, *Journey Through the City*. Ask readers to point to the words with long /e/ sounds. Help them practice blending the sounds in *city*. Have students take a quick look through the first few pages of text to identify and decode additional words with long /e/ sounds, including *key*, *many*, and *alley*.

During Reading:

- Have readers point under each word as they read it.
- **Decoding:** If readers are stuck on a word, help them say each sound and blend the sounds together smoothly. You may want to point out words with *y* and *ey* as they appear.
- **Comprehension:** Invite students to talk about what new things they are learning about cities while reading. What are they learning that they didn't know before?

After Reading:

Discuss the book. Some ideas for questions:

- What places do you visit in your community? Why do you visit those places?
- What do you still wonder about places in cities?

Journey Through the City

Text by Marley Richmond

Reading Consultant
Deborah MacPhee, PhD
Professor, School of Teaching and Learning
Illinois State University

PICTURE WINDOW BOOKS
a capstone imprint

Let’s take a journey through the city!

Get ready for the journey!

Use a key to lock your home when you leave.

In the city, lots of homes are close together.

Many people live
in neighborhoods.

An alley runs between these homes.

Cars drive
through the alley.

This home has a chimney.

This one has a yard where a puppy runs!

A city has lots of stores. It can have candy shops. People buy sweets and ice cream here.

Some candy is made with honey. Yum!

A city can have a bank.

People keep their money in banks. Banks can also lend people money.

This city has a zoo
with lots of animals.

If you go to the zoo, you might see a monkey, a lion, or a donkey!

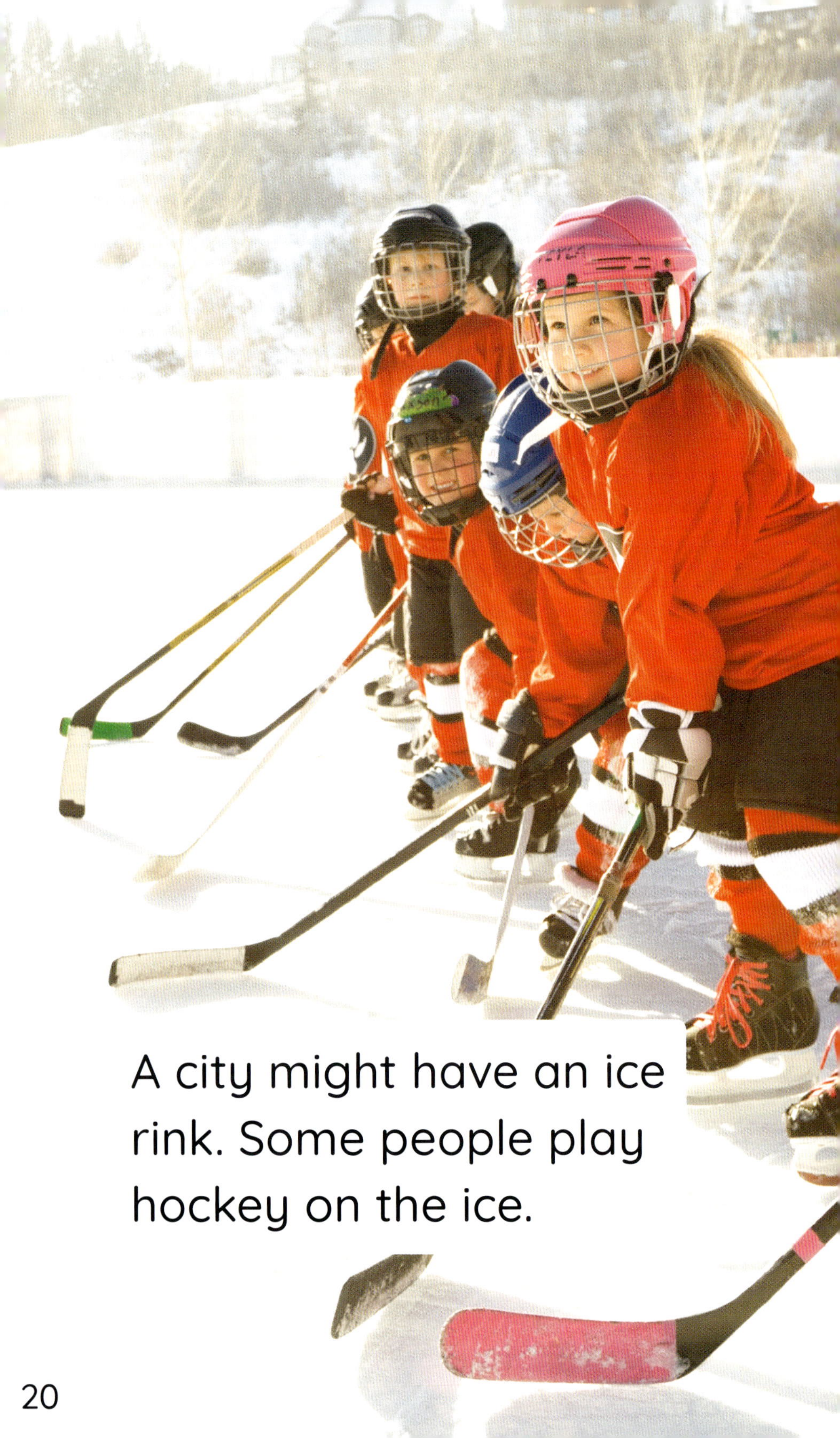

A city might have an ice rink. Some people play hockey on the ice.

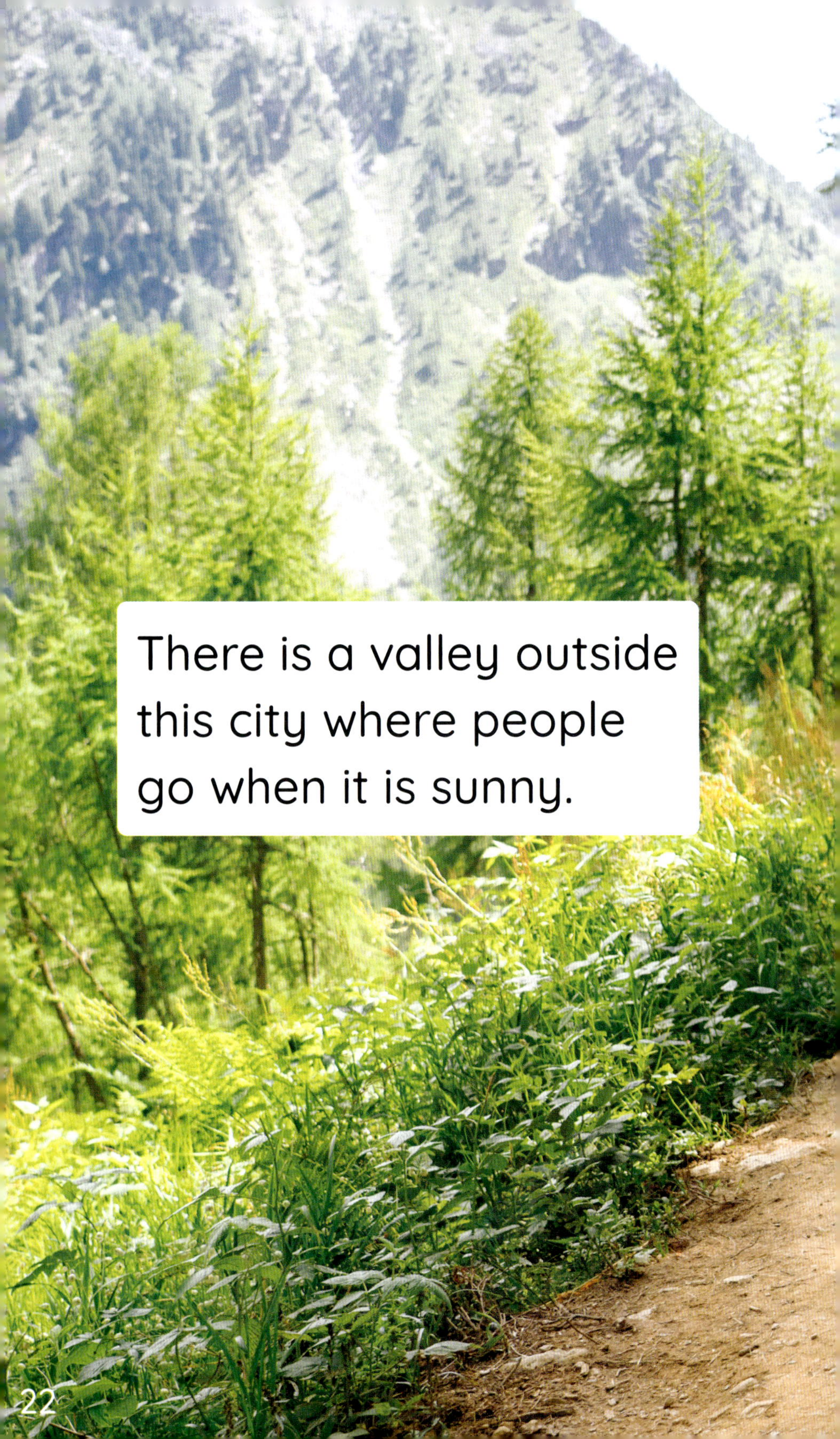

There is a valley outside this city where people go when it is sunny.

Put on a coat if it is windy. Wear boots if it is muddy.

A city might have a community center.

This is a place for people to gather.

Kids can play games at a community center.

Adults have meetings there to make plans and rules for the city.

There are lots of fun things to do in a city. Now it's time for your next journey!

More Ideas:

Phonics and Phonemic Awareness Activity

Matching Vowel Patterns:
Prepare word cards with long /e/ vowel patterns. Words could include *y* or *ey*. Place the cards on a workspace. Ask readers to make pairs of words that use the same vowel pattern to make the long /e/ sound. Have readers sound out each pair of words and compare the long vowel sound each vowel pattern makes.

Suggested words:
y: puppy, city, candy, windy, muddy, sunny
ey: key, alley, chimney, honey, money, monkey, donkey, hockey, valley

Extended Learning Activity

Take Your Own Journey:
Cities can include all kinds of places. Ask readers to imagine they are taking a trip through a city. What kinds of places would they find? What would they do in the city? How would they get around? Ask readers to write a few sentences describing their journey through the imaginary city. Challenge them to use words with the long vowel sound /e/ spelled *y* or *ey*.

Published by Picture Window Books, an imprint of Capstone
1710 Roe Crest Drive, North Mankato, Minnesota 56003
capstonepub.com

Library of Congress Cataloging-in-Publication Data is available on the Library of Congress website.

ISBN: 9798875277702 (hardback)
ISBN: 9798875277665 (paperback)
ISBN: 9798875277641 (eBook PDF)

Image Credits: Getty: Dee Liu, front cover, FamVeld, 18, FG Trade, 14, Fly View Productions, 17, JLco - Julia Amaral, 6, kate_sept2004, 7, Koto, 27, mbbirdy, 28, Pgiam, 16, Wirestock, 13; Shutterstock: ABCDstock, 2–3, EQRoy, 15, Eric Isselee, 19, Hero Images Inc, 20–21, Irina WS, 4–5, back cover, Kristi Blokhin, 8–9, 32, Monkey Business Images, 29, OlenaPalaguta, 22–23, Steve Cukrov, 26, Stockr, 1, 30–31, Susan Law Cain, 12, Trong Nguyen, 10–11, ur72, 24–25

Printed and bound in China. PO 6460